Photoline

Book of photo memories

Nikolas Ker

Instruction

Photo line Book describes all the person that make trips and met new events, places, amazing landscapes in their trips and also magical moments that had pictures . This book describes the ordinary person who travels and knows new places and immortalizes the memories. All the photos in this album photographed by me or helped to make them. I traveled In 28 countries in Asia , Europe and American Continent and this book some of them. I hope to like it...

Landscape from Czesc Republic by Plane

Landscape from Bucharest by plane

Landscape from Greece by plane

Landscape from Bulgaria by Ryanair plane

Landscape from England by Plane

The beautiful sky from Scotland by plane

Pictures from Ireland outside from Dublin in nature

Nikolas Ker

15

Sky from Poland – Lodz in day

Sunrise from Greece – Delphi

Rainbow from Scotland in fort Augustus village during the day

Sky and buildings in Poland-Warsaw

Dawn in Slovakia - Bajerov

Day in Slovakia – Bajerov castle

Sunrise in Polish park

Romania - Bucharest in Winter by snow (Sector 6)

Bucharest sky with buildings in the evening

Landscape from Bucharest by plane

Sunrise in Romexpo in Bucharest

Passenger ships in Poland - Gdansk

Big Ben in London

London by Night – Big Ben

Greece during the day in Kos Island

Greece in Rhodes Island

Candles in the temple Bucharest

Plaza Romana in Bucharest

Sunrise in Bucharest

Sky with birds in Bucharest

Sky in Bucharest Park Herastrau

Bucharest in winter (sector 6)

Church in Piata Unirii Bucharest

Butterfly in Sweden - Stockholm

Tower in Peru

Snowman and showgirl in Bucharest

Church in Poland – Lodz

Modern Bucharest

Greece - mountain slope with sea

Greece Athens – Theatrical play (Electra)

Greece - Igoumenitsa sea

Bucharest – The fallen building

Greece – Nafplio

Poland – Warsaw Independent day

Metro in Bucharest

Bucharest with iced trees

Moon in Romanian sky

Fallen sky in Bucharest

Romania – Brasov in winter

Romania – Sibiu Mountain

Garden in the center of Bucharest

Cat with certain

Prodigy in Untold Cluj – Romania

Untold Festival in Cluj – Romania

Prodigy's singer in Cluj (Untold Festival)

Swan in Bucharest park

Theatrical Play in Athens

View with boat from Veranda edge

Cake in Switzerland

Cat with lights in France – Marseille

Ukraine girl is photographed

Photographed in the museum of senses

Poland – Warsaw in Winter Palace Cultury

Swan in the park

Cloudy veil in France

Romania – Tineretului park

When the plane is ready to leave from Warsaw – Modlin Airport

Landscape from Oslo in Norway by plane

47

Greek Landscape from parachute

Japan Saitama Castle

Japan – Saitama material for food

Japan – Saitama streets

Poland – Krakow night in Wawel Castle

Plane is shy

Amsterdam by evening

Morning in , Kwintesencja Netherlands

Adventure in Skocjan Caves Slovenia

Austria – Wien in museum of water nature

Austria- Wien museum of water nature

Austria – Wien National Stadium

Lithuania – Vilnius in Winter

Italy – Venetia early morning

Italy - Building with construction site

USA - Chicago moonlight with the river

9 781798 748299